A Girl Named
Misty

The True Story of
MISTY COPELAND

By **Kelly Starling Lyons**

Illustrated by **Melissa Manwill**

Scholastic Inc.

The story on pages 47-48 first appeared in *American Girl* magazine in the July/August 2016 issue, page 5.

Photos ©: 43: Kevin Karzin/AP Images; 44 top: Andrea Mohin/The New York Times/Redux; 44 bottom left: Alastair Muir/REX/Shutterstock; 44 bottom right: Hiroyuki Ito/Getty Images; 45: Andrea Mohin/The New York Times/Redux; 46 left: Gary Gershoff/Getty Images; 46 top: Kevin Mazur/Getty Images; 46 bottom: Henry Leutwyler/Getty Images; 47: Jorge Narvaez.

Book design by Suzanne LaGasa

Library of Congress Cataloging-in-Publication Number: 2017049440

americangirl.com/service

ISBN 978-1-338-19305-3

10 9 8 7 6 5   19 20 21 22

Printed in the U.S.A.   23
First printing 2018

Contents

Introduction

Misty Copeland loved to dance. Growing up, Misty was a shy African American girl who blended into the background of her big family. Little did she know that one day she would be a star. From the start, the passion inside Misty shone through each twirl and leap. Dancing made her feel free and strong. This quiet little girl's talent would lead her to become a groundbreaking dancer at one of the top ballet companies in the world.

Chapter 1

Finding Her Shine

Change was part of Misty's childhood. Born on September 10, 1982, in Kansas City, Missouri, she moved with her mom, Sylvia DelaCerna, and siblings to Southern California when she was two. Over the years, they moved between apartments and houses. Sometimes Misty's family had to make do with little money.

With two big brothers, a big sister, and a younger brother and sister, Misty had to share her mom's attention. Misty lit up when her mom complimented something she had done. She pushed herself to be perfect in school, but worries nagged her. What if her best wasn't good enough? What if they moved again?

At home in San Pedro, California, seven-year-old Misty was watching TV when a movie about Olympic **gymnast** Nadia Comaneci came on. Her flips, spins, and leaps across the floor amazed Misty. Watching Nadia's mix of **acrobatics** and dance made her want to move like that, too.

In the yard, Misty taught herself how to do cartwheels and handstands. She was able to master gymnastic moves with little effort. Misty pretended to perform for an audience and imagined their roaring applause when she did all her moves just right.

Something special filled Misty's heart when she heard Mariah Carey songs, too. She felt a connection to Mariah, who was biracial like she was. Misty's mom and dad were both half black and half white. Seeing someone who looked like her being successful and achieving her own dream inspired Misty.

When Misty made up dances in her bedroom, she was able to act out the words and feelings as the music flowed through her. It was like a light flipped on inside her and she began to shine. Misty's worries about school, money, and where they lived disappeared as she danced.

Chapter 2

Stepping Out

In middle school, Misty set a huge goal that would change her life. She wanted to earn a spot on the **drill team**—a type of dance group. And not just any spot. Misty was determined to be captain.

Her big sister, Erica, had been a star on that same team. Her mom had been a professional cheerleader. Could Misty, the girl who was afraid to read aloud in class, really become the leader of the group?

On audition day, Misty stepped in front of the judges and gave it her all. She not only became captain but caught the eye of Coach Elizabeth Cantine, who had studied ballet. As Coach Cantine watched Misty during practice and at shows, she knew Misty had a gift.

Coach Cantine told Misty a friend of hers was teaching ballet at the San Pedro Boys & Girls Club. Misty was nervous about taking the class. After school, she sat on the bleachers at the Boys & Girls Club, watching other children learn basic ballet steps. For two weeks, she just sat there. Not even the ballet teacher's encouragement could get her to join in.

Then one day, Misty changed into a T-shirt, shorts, and socks and decided to give ballet a chance. Surrounded by kids wearing **leotards** and tights, she felt out of place. Misty was usually confident when she danced, but not

this time. The moves made her feel awkward and insecure. By the end of the class, she'd had enough. Misty decided her time with ballet was done.

Chapter 3

Putting in the Work

Cindy Bradley, who taught the ballet class at the Boys & Girls Club, had other plans. From the beginning, she saw Misty's talent. She convinced her to come back. At age thirteen, Misty was much older than most beginners, but she was a natural. Cindy offered Misty a full **scholarship** to her ballet school so she could learn more. All of her classes and ballet clothes would be free. Misty's mom was so proud of her daughter for earning a chance to develop her talent.

Almost every day, Misty went to Cindy's studio. The classes were grueling and required a lot of focus, but every step, leap, and spin filled Misty with joy. Soon, Misty was excelling— nothing could stop her. Just two months after starting ballet lessons, Misty went **en pointe**— on the tips of her toes. Dancing en pointe is a skill that takes most dancers years to master.

Cindy told Misty she was perfect for ballet. She could perform moves easily that usually take a lot of training and practice. She had a ballerina's form. Misty knew in her heart ballet was where she belonged.

Meanwhile, life at home was getting harder. Misty's family had to find another place to live and had moved into a motel room. Her sister Erica took the long bus ride with Misty from Cindy's studio back to their home. Between school, her daily ballet practice, and long bus rides, Misty was gone a lot.

Misty's mom worried that Misty was away from her family and friends too much. Her mom said Misty had to give up ballet.

Chapter 4

The Making of a Star

Misty was devastated at the thought of not taking ballet anymore. She told Cindy the news. Cindy asked Misty's mom if Misty could live with Cindy's family during the week so

that Misty would be close to the studio. Misty would go home every weekend. It was a tough decision, but Misty's mom agreed.

At Cindy's studio, Misty got better and better. She mastered every move and took advanced classes, pushing herself to be the best. People called her a **prodigy**—a young person with amazing skill. She watched ballet on TV and carried dance magazines in her backpack. Ballet was her life.

Though she loved ballet, Misty had never actually seen a live performance until Cindy took her to see *Don Quixote* (kee-ho-tee). At just nineteen, the star of the show, Paloma Herrera, had become a **principal** dancer at American Ballet Theatre (ABT) in New York City. ABT was one of the top ballet companies, or performing groups, in the world. Misty watched Paloma and dreamed of being an ABT principal dancer, too.

Meanwhile, Misty's mom and siblings cheered as she dazzled audiences with her performances, like in *The Nutcracker* and *The Chocolate Nutcracker*.

Becoming a great ballerina meant working long hours. Some weekends Misty didn't have time to come home. That upset her mom. She loved Misty and wanted her to be happy and keep dancing, but felt she should be spending more time with her family. Cindy also loved her and wanted her to keep living and training with her. Misty felt torn apart.

Chapter 5

City of Dreams

In time, it was decided Misty would live with her mom and siblings and go to a different ballet studio closer to home. After a while, Misty's mom got a new job and moved her family from the motel to a nice apartment. Misty worked hard at the new ballet studio and even earned an invitation to a summer program at American Ballet Theatre!

Misty's dedication and talent wowed the people at ABT. The next year, after Misty graduated from high school, she moved to New York City to become a member of ABT—the same company that her idol, Paloma Herrera, danced for.

Walking around the busy streets of New York, Misty saw a beautiful mix of people of different races and backgrounds living and working together. But inside ABT, she saw

something else. When she was promoted, at age nineteen, to the **corps de ballet**—a permanent member of the main ballet company—Misty was the only black woman out of dozens of dancers.

Shortly after joining the corps de ballet, Misty felt a terrible pain while dancing. She injured her back and would need a year to recover. When Misty returned to ABT, she had changed. Her thin body had matured and had more curves, a shape some thought wasn't right for ballet.

It hurt Misty to know that some people didn't think women with brown skin and curves should be ballerinas. Over time, other African Americans in the world of ballet helped Misty see that she belonged. She was not just dancing for herself anymore. She was dancing for every African American ballerina who never had a chance to rise to the top. She danced for all the kids who would one day follow her example. Misty found strength in them and in herself.

Chapter 6

Dancing in the Spotlight

Misty showed everyone she deserved the spotlight. At the age of twenty-four she became a **soloist**. Misty was only the second African American female soloist in the company's history.

Five years later, she got the role of a lifetime in *The Firebird*. This famous ballet, about a magical bird who helps a prince defeat an evil sorcerer, had been around for more than one hundred years. Misty would be the first African American woman to dance the role of the Firebird for a major ballet company.

Not only did Misty come back to ABT, three years after her performance as the Firebird, the artistic **director** of ABT told Misty Copeland to take a bow. She had been promoted to principal dancer—the highest level a dancer can reach. Misty had finally achieved her dream. She was the first African American female principal dancer in the company's history. As her ABT family cheered for her, she could feel the world applauding, too. Misty, the shy little girl with the big talent, had become the star she was always meant to be.

GLOSSARY

ACROBATICS: difficult gymnastic moves

CORPS DE BALLET: a permanent member of a ballet company

DIRECTOR: the person in charge

DRILL TEAM: a type of dance group

EN POINTE: dancing on the tips of the toes

FRACTURE: to break or crack something, especially a bone

GYMNAST: a person who performs difficult and carefully controlled body movements

LEOTARD: a tight one-piece garment worn for dancing or exercise

PRINCIPAL: most important, chief, or main

PRODIGY: an extremely smart or talented young person

SCHOLARSHIP: a grant or prize that pays for someone to go to college or follow a course of study

SOLOIST: person who performs on her own

TIMELINE

1982: Misty Copeland is born in Kansas City, Missouri, on September 10

1985: Misty moves to San Pedro, California, with her mom and siblings

1989–1990: Misty begins trying gymnastic moves at home after watching a movie about Olympic gymnast Nadia Comaneci

1995: Cindy Bradley offers Misty a full scholarship to her ballet school

Sixteen-year-old Misty Copeland poses at the Lauridsen Ballet Center in California in 1998.

TOP: Misty performing in *The Sleeping Beauty* at the Metropolitan Opera House in 2013. LEFT: Misty dancing in 2011 with ABT in *Company B* in London. RIGHT: Misty performing *Don Quixote* in 2017.

1996: Misty dances en pointe after only two months of classes

1996: Misty performs the lead role of Clara in *The Nutcracker* ballet

2000: Misty is invited to participate in a summer program at American Ballet Theatre

2001: Misty is promoted to ABT's corps de ballet at age nineteen

2007: Misty becomes a soloist at age twenty-four

2012: Misty performs the lead role in *The Firebird* at the Metropolitan Opera House in June, the first African American dancer to be cast in that part for a major ballet company

2012: Misty's injuries require major surgery in October

Misty returned as the Firebird in 2016, four years after her initial performance.

2015: Misty is promoted to principal dancer at ABT, the first African American woman in the history of the company

TOP: Misty is honored at the Time 100 Gala celebrating the "100 Most Influential People in the World" on April 21, 2015. RIGHT: Misty is photographed in 2016.

A GIRL NAMED ALEXA

There are a lot of young girls helping to make positive changes in our world today, just like Misty Copeland did. Alexa Narvaez is one of those girls.

It all started with a song. My dad and I love to sing together. One time when I was little, my dad shared one of our songs online for my cousins to see. If you can believe it, more than 30 million people have watched that first video. Now I'm 13 years old with a baby brother and my dad and I are still making videos every week. We have now had more than 210 million views on our songs! Over the years, we've been invited to sing in places like China, Canada, and Australia. And even on a popular TV show here in the US! It's fun to sing in front of people, and I love singing with my dad.

When I was younger, I was bullied a lot. Not all the comments on our videos are good, but seeing the good comments inspires me and gives me good vibes. Singing has helped me to learn to like myself more. If I'm having a bad day, I'll sing a happy song. It makes me feel good, and strong, and gives me hope. The best part of this experience has been making myself and other people happy through my music. I hope our videos are helping other people believe in themselves and inspiring them to find something that they love to do.